MW00452143

The Boar's Head Festival

Merry Christmas, Lila ~
Love, Grandad & Nana 2018

In 2017, you visited The Boar's Head!

The Boar's Head Festival

A Christmas Celebration

LaLonnie Lehman

LaLonnie Lehman
Illustrated by Susan J. Halbower

To Lila Lorraine
I hope you love
the Boar's Head Festival!
LaLonnie

Library of Congress Cataloging-in-Publication Data

Lehman, LaLonnie, author.
  The Boar's Head Festival : a Christmas celebration / LaLonnie Lehman ; illustrated by Susan J.
Halbower.
      pages cm
  Summary: "A heavily illustrated volume for children and adults that tells the story of the
Boar's Head Festival, a Christmas celebration incorporating such medieval legends as that of
Good King Wenceslas, the boar's head legend in which a ferocious boar is killed by a young
Oxford scholar, and the Nativity story. The celebration is narrated and played out by beautifully
costumed actors in medieval garb."--ECIP Summary.
  ISBN 978-0-87565-626-7 (alk. paper)
  1. Boar's Head and Yule Log Festival. 2. Christmas plays, American--Texas--Fort Worth. 3.
Winter festivals--Texas--Fort Worth. 4. Winter festivals--Texas--Fort Worth--Juvenile literature.
I. Halbower, Susan J., illustrator. II. Title.
  GT4986.T4L45 2015
  394.2663--dc23
                          2015031173

TCU Press
TCU Box 298300
Fort Worth, Texas 76129
817.257.7822
www.prs.tcu.edu

To order books: 1.800.826.8911

To all who have made the Boar's Head and Yule Log Festival
at University Christian Church in Fort Worth possible,
and especially to those who, with me, initiated
the festival at UCC in the early 1970s—Penny Pennybacker,
Ralph Stone, Ken Lawrence, and Hank Hammack.

Thanks to my family for their enduring support,
my husband Wayne for his patience,
and my friend Linda Peckham for her
continued encouragement and wisdom.
My appreciation to Susan Halbower for her illustrations,
which brought this story to life,
and the staff at TCU Press who faithfully
guided my idea into this book.

—LaLonnie Lehman

For my parents and grandparents, all devoted churchgoers,
and for Jay, who lives the magic of Christmas.

—Susan Halbower

About This Book

The stories in this book are from secular and religious traditions. Drawings are based on medieval architecture and illuminated manuscripts. The costumes illustrated are based on those used in the Boar's Head and Yule Log Festival, presented annually at University Christian Church, Fort Worth, Texas. The festival, first presented in 1975, continues to this day.

Introduction

Many stories are told or sung over and over until
they become well known.
Certain ones are performed to celebrate
special seasons or special events
like Christmas, and the stories and songs become
a part of those events.
This is true of the stories that are told and sung
in the Boar's Head Festival. They are folktales and
songs that originated in medieval times and helped
celebrate the winter solstice and the beginning
of the New Year.
Churches used the folktales and songs to teach
about Christianity, and soon they added the story
of the birth of Jesus. By the 1400s, those songs
and stories had become a celebration called the
Boar's Head and Yule Log Festival.
This ancient festival has continued to be performed
to the present time.
Come, read the stories!

The Story of the Boar's Head

A student was sitting in the woods near Oxford, England,
reading his book. It was written by a wise Greek man
named Aristotle.
When the student heard a noise, he looked up and saw a
wild boar running right at him.
He leaped up. What could he do?
He had only his book for a weapon. He thrust the book
into the open mouth of the boar, killing him.
Then he ran back to the village and told his story.
The Lord of the Manor declared, "Everyone in the village
must come to the manor house and praise the student
for overcoming the beast with his quick thinking."
"Let's have a party to celebrate!" cried the village people.
"We will have it during the winter solstice!"
And so on the night in December when the day is the
shortest and the night the longest, a huge feast was held to
celebrate the triumph of good over evil,
of light over darkness.
That gathering became a Yuletide tradition, a celebration
that brightens the darkest winter days of the year.

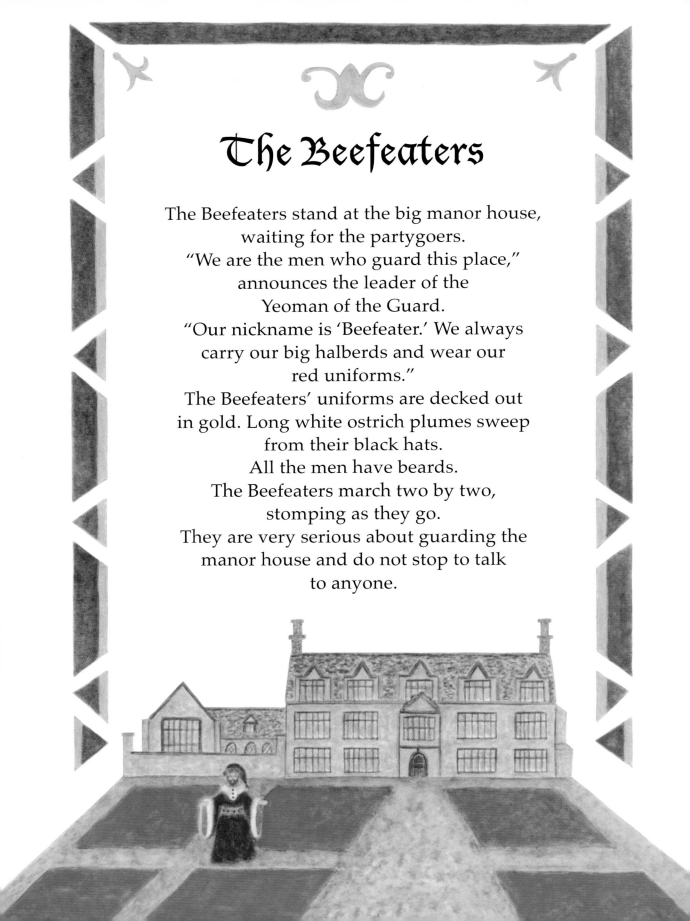

The Beefeaters

The Beefeaters stand at the big manor house,
waiting for the partygoers.
"We are the men who guard this place,"
announces the leader of the
Yeoman of the Guard.
"Our nickname is 'Beefeater.' We always
carry our big halberds and wear our
red uniforms."
The Beefeaters' uniforms are decked out
in gold. Long white ostrich plumes sweep
from their black hats.
All the men have beards.
The Beefeaters march two by two,
stomping as they go.
They are very serious about guarding the
manor house and do not stop to talk
to anyone.

The Procession

In great merriment, the villagers
gather to parade to the big
manor house.
The herald leads the villagers,
singing a rousing song
about the boar.
His attendants follow along,
holding up banners for the party. The song tells
the villagers that they should be merry, not alarmed.

Four men boost the boar's head on
a trencher. It is decorated with gay garlands.
The men bearing the trencher beckon to the
other people from the village.
"Follow us," they call out.

The loud hunters arrive next. "We bring meat from our hunt!" they shout.
"Mince pie will be our treat," some young men say.
Other young men proclaim, "We have plum pudding!"
The cooks come loaded down with bread, wine, cheese, and vegetables.

The ladies of the manor wear their prettiest jewels and their best gowns, made of the finest silk and velvet.
"Welcome to the festival," they say to all.

Young girls appear,
prancing and bowing.
"We have gathered holly for decorations."
"We can dance!" some giggling
girls say, twirling.
The littlest children pretend to be sprites.
"Do we look like sprites?" they ask,
skipping happily.

"We have cut the tree for the Yule log," the woodsmen announce.
"Here comes the Yule log! Here comes the Yule log!" the boys chant.
"Put it in the fireplace," directs the Lord of the Manor.
"We will light it with a piece of last year's Yule log. It will burn for
twelve days and bring good luck for the New Year."

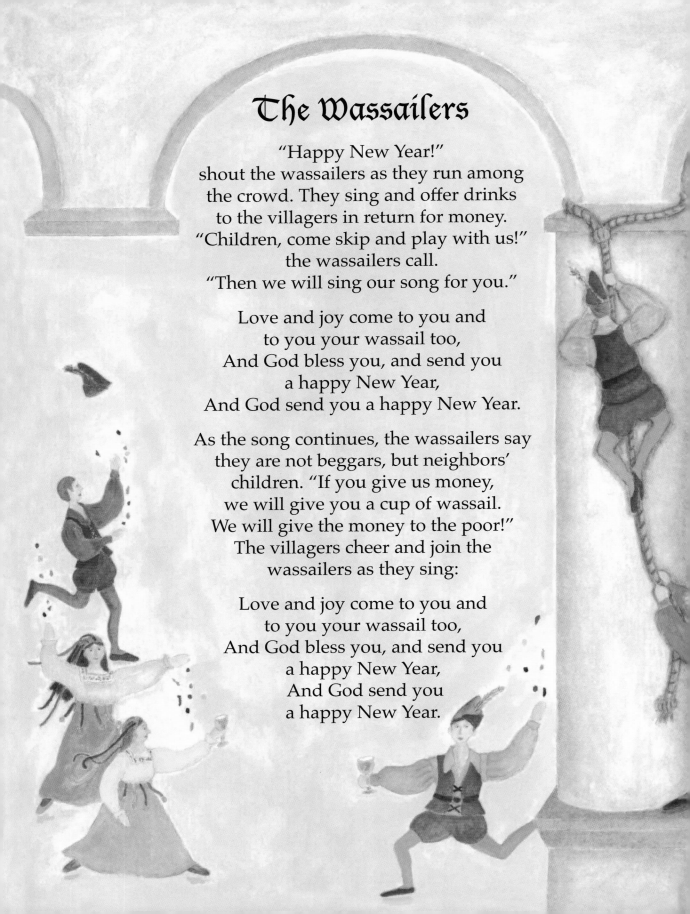

The Wassailers

"Happy New Year!"
shout the wassailers as they run among
the crowd. They sing and offer drinks
to the villagers in return for money.
"Children, come skip and play with us!"
the wassailers call.
"Then we will sing our song for you."

Love and joy come to you and
to you your wassail too,
And God bless you, and send you
a happy New Year,
And God send you a happy New Year.

As the song continues, the wassailers say
they are not beggars, but neighbors'
children. "If you give us money,
we will give you a cup of wassail.
We will give the money to the poor!"
The villagers cheer and join the
wassailers as they sing:

Love and joy come to you and
to you your wassail too,
And God bless you, and send you
a happy New Year,
And God send you
a happy New Year.

King Wenceslas

Good King Wenceslas and his two pages look out at
the cold and snowy night.
It is December 26, the feast of Saint Stephen.
They see a man in a tattered, thin cloak.
"Who is that poor man?" King Wenceslas asks.
"Where is his house?"
"He lives far from here," the first page answers.
"Next to the mountain by the forest fence
near Saint Agnes's fountain."
King Wenceslas tells his pages,
"Bring me meat and wine."
He looks out again and adds,
"And get some logs for a fire.
We will give the poor man food and fuel."
As soon as the supplies are gathered,
the king and his pages start out to follow the man.
The load is heavy and the pages get cold.
"Walk behind me," King Wenceslas says,
and the pages discover that walking in the
footsteps of the king gives them warmth.
By caring for the poor man,
the king and his pages are blessed.
"When people care for each other,"
King Wenceslas says, "all are blessed."

The Angel's Announcement

An angel appears in the evening sky to
speak to shepherds.
"Do not be afraid," the angel tells them.
"I bring you good news of great joy
for all people.
To you is born this day,
in the City of David,
a Savior who is Christ the Lord.
You will find him wrapped in swaddling
clothes and lying in a manger."
Then the heavens are filled with
a whole choir of angels singing
"Glory to God!"
The shepherds quickly herd
their sheep together.
"Let's do as the angel says!"
And they hurry to Bethlehem.

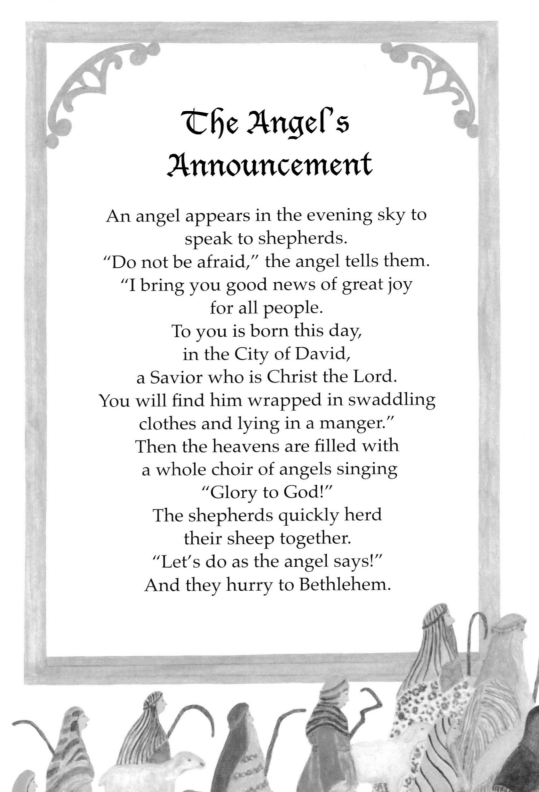

King Melchior, King Balthazar, and King Gaspar,
wise men from the East, have seen the star.
They realize that the star will lead them to the Messiah.

"The star leads to Bethlehem!" King Melchior exclaims
to the other kings.
Balthazar says, "We should take gifts."
Gaspar says, "We can take gold, and frankincense,
and myrrh."
"We should come, too," the kings' attendants say.
"We will carry the gifts."
Others go with them and
carry torches to light the way.

After the long journey
to Bethlehem,
the kings
and the shepherds
find the baby Jesus
in a manger.
The kings present
their gifts,
and all kneel down
in awe
to worship him.

The End

Boar's Head Carol

The boar's head in hand bear I,
Bedecked with bay and rosemary.
And I pray you, my masters, be merrie,
Quot estis in convivio.

Caput apri defero,
Reddens laudes Domino.

The boar's head, as I understand,
Is the bravest dish in all the land.
When thus bedecked with the gay garland,
Let us *servire cantico.*

Caput apri defero,
Reddens laudes Domino.

Our steward hath provided this,
In honor of the King of Bliss.
Which on this day to be served is,
In Reginensi atrio.

Caput apri defero,
Reddens laudes Domino.

—from a fifteenth-century English carol

The mightiest Hunter of them all,
We honor in this festal hall.
Born of a humble virgin mild,
Heaven's King became a helpless Child.

Caput apri defero,
Reddens laudes Domino.

He hunted down through earth and hell,
The swart boar death until it fell.
This mighty deed for us was done,
Therefore sing we in unison.

Caput apri defero,
Reddens laudes Domino.

Let not this boar's head cause alarm,
The Huntsman drew his power to harm.
So death, which still appears so grim,
Has yielded all its powers to Him!

Caput apri defero,
Reddens laudes Domino.

Glossary

Aristotle: A Greek philosopher, 384-322 BC.

Attendants: Like pages, they do special chores for their leaders.

Banners: Decorated flags or signs carried on long poles.

Beefeaters: Guards of the manor house.

Bethlehem: The name of the City of David in Judea.

Boar: A wild pig, usually with big tusks.

City of David: Bethlehem, the city in Judea where Jesus was born.

Festival: A grand party often featuring performances and usually celebrating a special event.

Glossary

Frankincense: A rare, sweet-smelling incense that comes from the sap of a tree and smells good when it is burned.

Halberd: A weapon with a sharp blade on a long pole.

Herald: An official messenger; a man who tells or sings a story with enthusiasm.

King Melchior, King Balthazar, King Gaspar: The three kings, called the Wise Men or the Magi, that followed the star to bring gifts to the baby Jesus.

King Wenceslas: In legend, he is the righteous king who does many good deeds for others. He is based on a real person: Vaclav, Duke of Bohemia, who achieved sainthood in the Catholic Church.

Ladies of the manor: Ladies who lived in the manor house.

Glossary

Lord of the Manor: In medieval times, he was the ruler of the village.

Manor house: The house of the village ruler, which had a big banquet hall for feasts and celebrations.

Messiah: Savior, the title of Jesus.

Mince pie: A pie made with raisins, apples, and spices.

Myrrh: Like frankincense, a sweet-smelling resin from a tree. It was used in perfumes and smells good when it is burned as incense.

Pages: Young people who do errands for their leader.

Plum pudding: A cake-like dessert containing spices and fruit.

Saint Agnes's fountain: A fountain near a monastery where Saint Agnes tended the sick.

Glossary

Shepherds: People who herd sheep.

Sprite: An elf or fairy.

Trencher: A platform with handles that is carried on the shoulders of four people.

Wassailers: Young men and women who beg for money to give to poor people.

Winter solstice: The shortest day of the year when the sun shines for only a few hours.

Yeomen of the Guard: A royal bodyguard formed by King Henry VII of England in 1485.

Yule log: The log that is added to the fireplace to start the New Year—to bring good luck to the household.

Yuletide: Christmastime.

About the Author

LALONNIE LEHMAN is Professor of Theatre at Texas Christian University. A costume historian and designer, she has designed costumes for theater, opera, ballet, modern dance, and musical and children's theater. She is a founding and continuing member of the Boar's Head and Yule Log Festival, now in its fortieth year, at University Christian Church, Fort Worth, Texas.

Memberships include the Costume Society of America and the United States Institute for Theatre Technology. Her book, *Fashion in the Time of The Great Gatsby*, Shire Publications, Ltd., London, was published in 2013.

About the Illustrator

SUSAN J. HALBOWER is a freelance artist with a degree in art from Kenyon College, Gambier, Ohio. She illustrated *Smurglets Are Everywhere*, a book of children's poetry, and *Log Cabin Kitty*, a pioneer history for children.